CONTENTS

Angels We Have Heard on High

Traditional French Carol
Translated by James Chadwick

Verse
Moderately

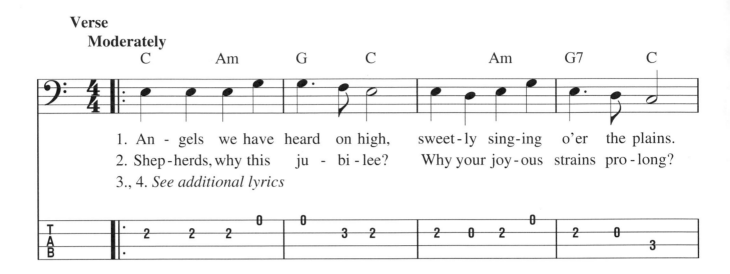

1. An - gels we have heard on high, sweet-ly sing-ing o'er the plains.
2. Shep-herds, why this ju - bi-lee? Why your joy-ous strains pro-long?
3., 4. *See additional lyrics*

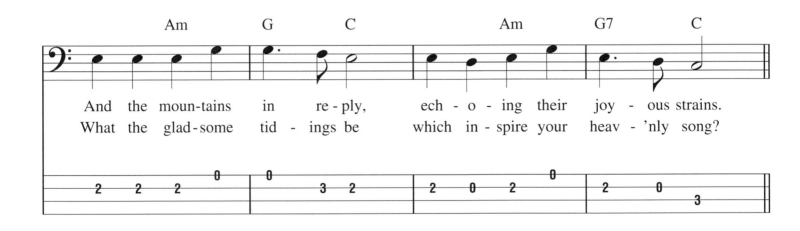

And the moun-tains in re-ply, ech - o - ing their joy - ous strains.
What the glad-some tid - ings be which in - spire your heav - 'nly song?

Chorus

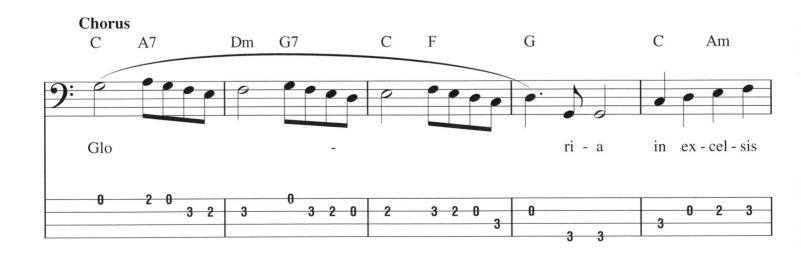

Glo - ri - a in ex - cel - sis

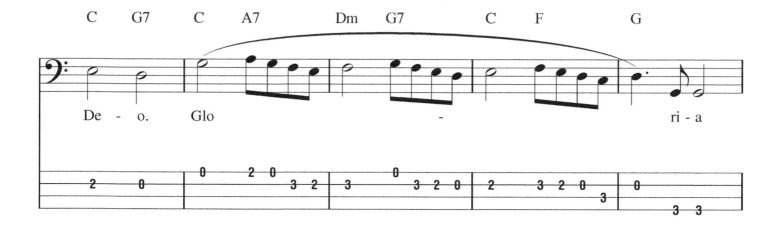

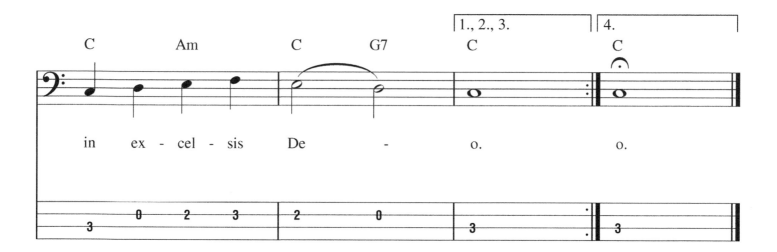

Additional Lyrics

3. Come to Bethlehem and See
   Him whose birth the angels sing;
   Come, adore on bended knee
   Christ the Lord, the Newborn King.

4. See within a manger laid
   Jesus, Lord of heaven and earth!
   Mary, Joseph, lend your aid,
   With us sing our Savior's birth.

Away in a Manger

Words by John T. McFarland (v.3)
Music by James R. Murray

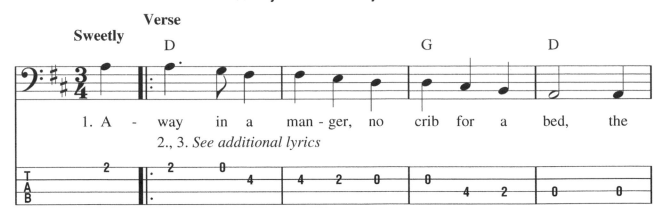

1. A - way in a man - ger, no crib for a bed, the
2., 3. *See additional lyrics*

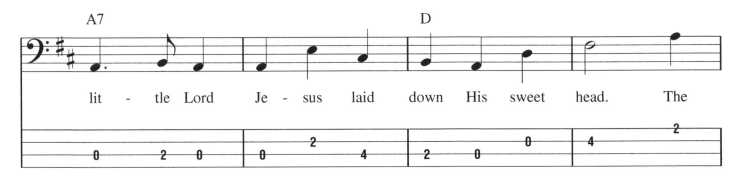

lit - tle Lord Je - sus laid down His sweet head. The

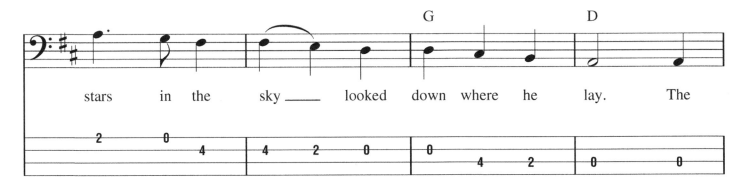

stars in the sky ____ looked down where he lay. The

lit - tle Lord Je - sus, a - sleep on the hay. 2. The there.

Additional Lyrics

2. The cattle are lowing, the baby awakes,
But little Lord Jesus, no crying He makes.
I love Thee, Lord Jesus, look down from the sky
And stay by my cradle till morning is nigh.

3. Be near me, Lord Jesus, I ask Thee to stay
Close by me forever and love me, I pray.
Bless all the dear children in Thy tender care
And fit us for heaven to live with Thee there.

Deck the Hall

Traditional Welsh Carol

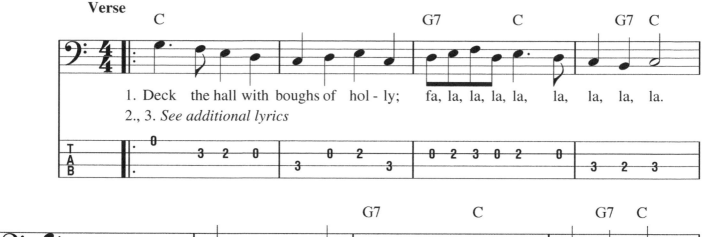

1. Deck the hall with boughs of hol - ly; fa, la, la, la, la, la, la, la, la.

2., 3. *See additional lyrics*

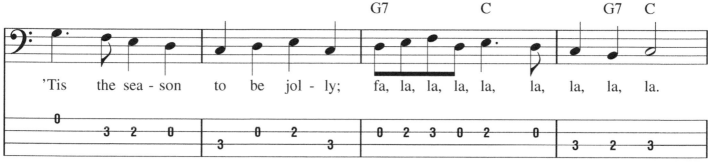

'Tis the sea - son to be jol - ly; fa, la, la, la, la, la, la, la, la.

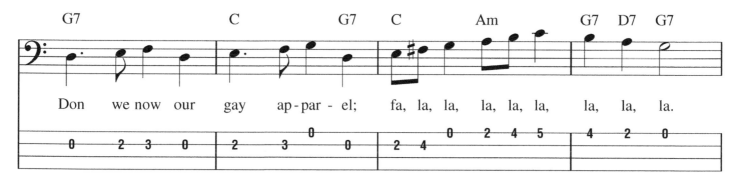

Don we now our gay ap - par - el; fa, la, la, la, la, la, la, la, la.

Troll the an - cient yule - tide car - ol; fa, la, la, la, la, la, la, la, la. la, la, la.

Additional Lyrics

2. See the blazing yule before us;
Fa, la, la, la, la, la, la, la, la.
Strike the harp and join the chorus;
Fa, la, la, la, la, la, la, la, la.
Follow me in merry measure;
Fa, la, la, la, la, la, la, la, la.
While I tell of Yuletide treasure;
Fa, la, la, la, la, la, la, la, la.

3. Fast away the old year passes;
Fa, la, la, la, la, la, la, la, la.
Hail the new ye lads and lasses;
Fa, la, la, la, la, la, la, la, la.
Sing we joyous, all together;
Fa, la, la, la, la, la, la, la, la.
Heedless of the wind and weather;
Fa, la, la, la, la, la, la, la, la, la.

Carol of the Bells

Ukrainian Christmas Carol

Moderately fast

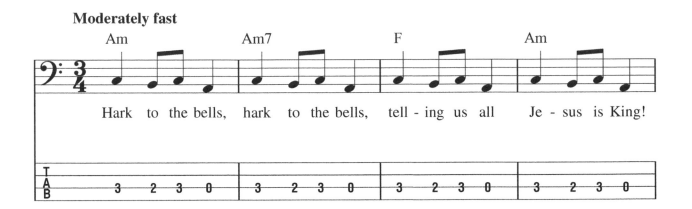

Hark to the bells, hark to the bells, tell - ing us all Je - sus is King!

Strong - ly they chime, sound with a rhyme, Christ - mas is here! Wel - come the King.

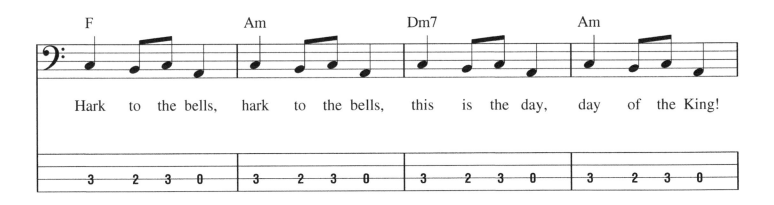

Hark to the bells, hark to the bells, this is the day, day of the King!

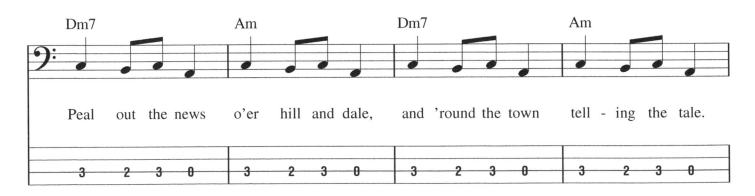

Peal out the news o'er hill and dale, and 'round the town tell - ing the tale.

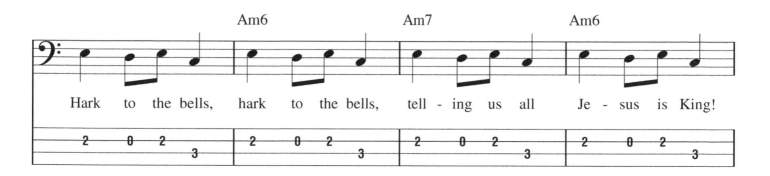

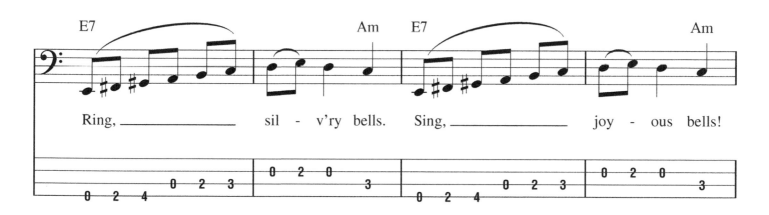

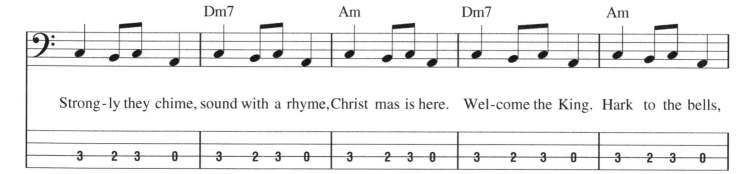

9

The First Noël

17th Century English Carol
Music from W. Sandys' *Christmas Carols*

Verse
Moderately slow

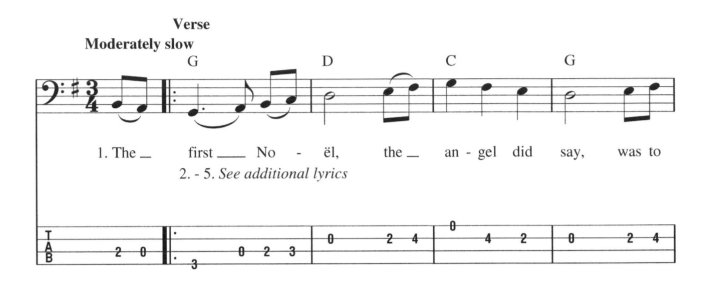

1. The _ first _ No - ël, the _ an - gel did say, was to
2. - 5. *See additional lyrics*

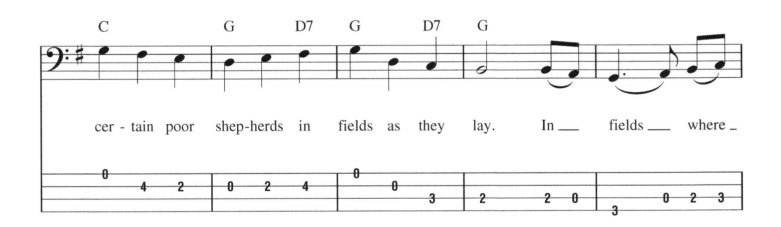

cer - tain poor shep-herds in fields as they lay. In _ fields _ where _

they lay _ keep - ing their sheep, on a cold win - ter's night _ that

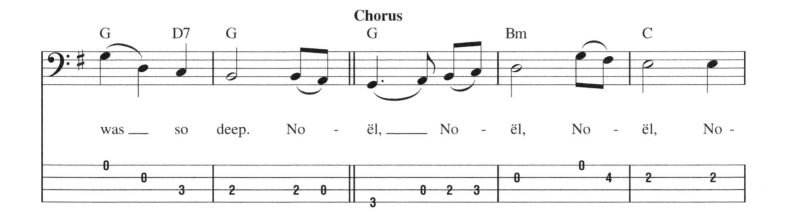

Chorus

was — so deep. No - ël, — No - ël, No - ël, No -

ël, born is the King — of Is - ra - el. 2. They — el.

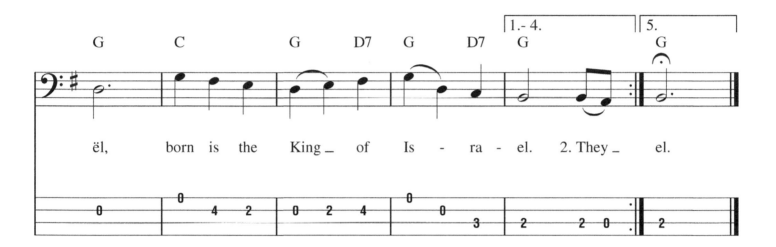

Additional Lyrics

2. They looked up and saw a star
   Shining in the east, beyond them far.
   And to the earth it gave great light
   And so it continued both day and night.

3. And by the light of that same star,
   Three wise men came from country far;
   To seek for a King was their intent,
   And to follow the star wherever it went.

4. This star drew nigh to the northwest,
   O'er Bethlehem it took its rest;
   And there it did both stop and say,
   Right over the place where Jesus lay.

5. Then entered in those wise men three,
   Full reverently upon their knee;
   And offered there in His presence,
   Their gold, and myrrh, and frankincense.

Go, Tell It on the Mountain

African-American Spiritual
Verses by John W. Work, Jr.

Additional Lyrics

2. The shepherds feared and trembled
   When, lo! above the earth
   Rang out the angel chorus
   That hailed our Savior's birth.

3. Down in a lowly manger
   Our humble Christ was born.
   And God sent us salvation
   That blessed Christmas morn.

Jolly Old St. Nicholas

Traditional 19th Century American Carol

Additional Lyrics

2. When the clock is striking twelve, when I'm fast asleep,
   Down the chimney broad and black, with your pack you'll creep.
   All the stockings you will find hanging in a row.
   Mine will be the shortest one, you'll be sure to know.

3. Johnny wants a pair of skates; Suzy wants a sled.
   Nellie wants a picture book, yellow, blue and red.
   Now I think I'll leave to you what to give the rest.
   Choose for me, dear Santa Claus, you will know the best.

God Rest Ye Merry, Gentlemen

19th Century English Carol

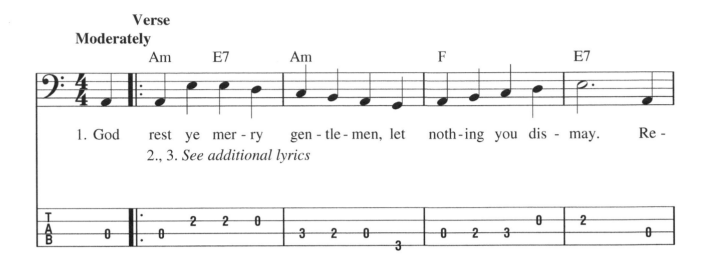

1. God rest ye mer - ry gen - tle - men, let noth - ing you dis - may. Re -
2., 3. *See additional lyrics*

mem - ber Christ our Sav - iour was born on Christ - mas day to

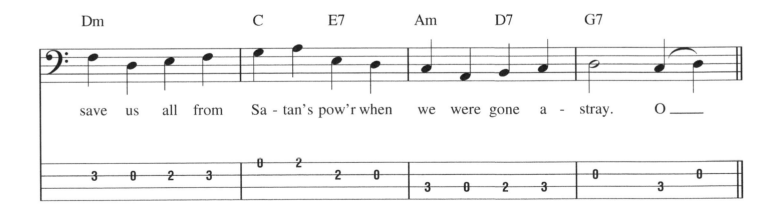

save us all from Sa - tan's pow'r when we were gone a - stray. O ___

Chorus

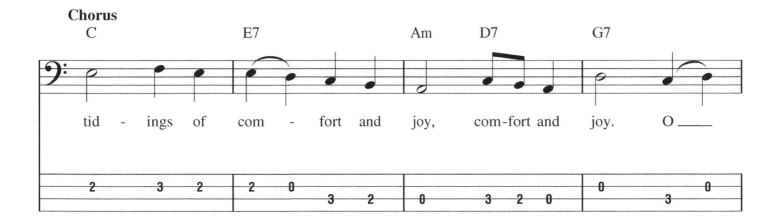

tid - ings of com - fort and joy, com-fort and joy. O____

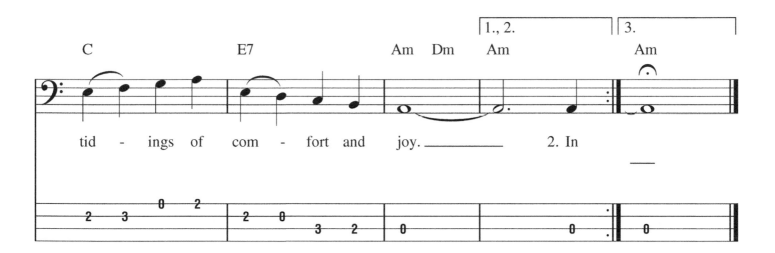

tid - ings of com - fort and joy._____ 2. In

Additional Lyrics

2. In Bethlehem, in Jewry,
This blessed babe was born,
And laid within a manger
Upon this blessed morn
That which His mother Mary
Did nothing take in scorn.

3. From God, our Heav'nly Father,
A blessed angel came,
And unto certain shepherds
Brought tidings of the same.
How that in Bethlehem was born
The Son of God by name.

Good King Wenceslas

Words by John M. Neale
Music from *Piae Cantiones*

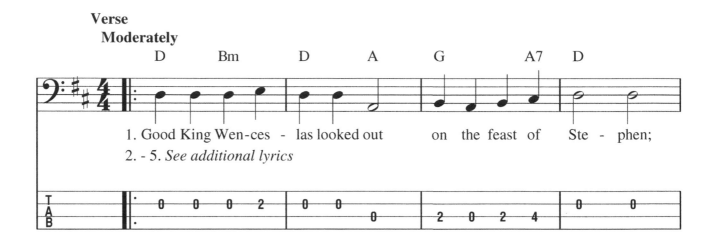

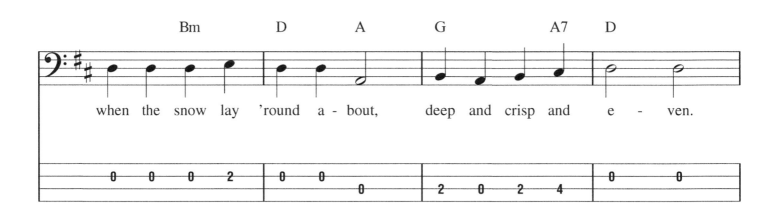

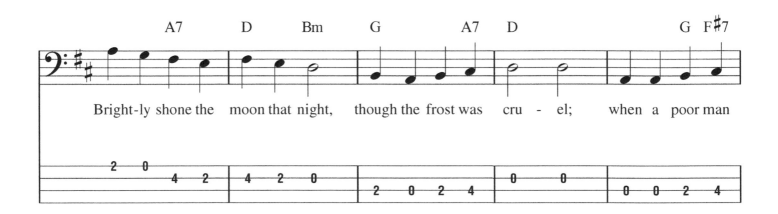

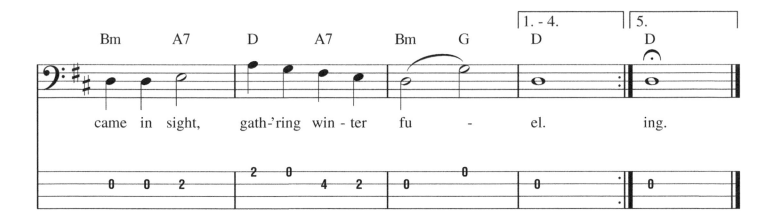

came in sight, gath-'ring win - ter fu - el. ing.

Additional Lyrics

2. "Hither page, and stand by me,
   If thou know'st it telling;
   Yonder peasent, who is he?
   Where and what his dwelling?"
   "Sire, he lives a good league hence,
   Underneath the mountain;
   Right against the forest fence,
   By Saint Agnes fountain."

3. "Bring me flesh, and bring me wine,
   Bring me pine-logs hither;
   Thou and I will see him dine,
   When we bear then thither."
   Page and monarch forth they went,
   Forth they went together;
   Through the rude winds wild lament,
   And the bitter weather.

4. "Sire, the night is darker now,
   And the wind blows stronger;
   Fails my heart, I know not how,
   I can go not longer."
   "Mark my footsteps, my good page,
   Tread thou in them boldly;
   Thou shalt find the winter's rage
   Freeze thy blood less coldly."

5. In his master's steps he trod,
   Where the snow lay dinted;
   Heat was in the very sod
   Which the saint has printed.
   Therefore, Christmas men, be sure,
   Wealth or rank posessing;
   Ye who now will bless the poor,
   Shall yourselves find blessing.

Hark! The Herald Angels Sing

Words by Charles Wesley
Altered by George Whitefield
Music by Felix Mendelssohn-Bartholdy
Arranged by William H. Cummings

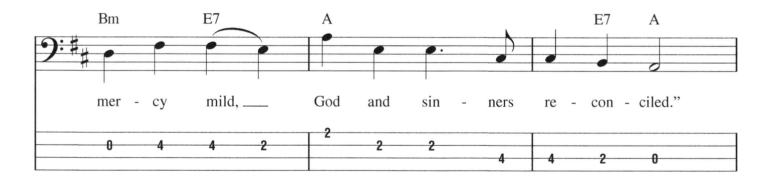

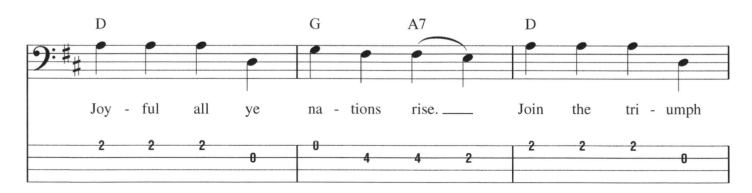

Additional Lyrics

2. Christ, by highest heav' adored, Christ, the everlasting Lord;
   Late in time behold Him come, offspring of the virgin's womb.
   Veil'd in flesh the Godhead see. Hail th'Incarnate Deity.
   Pleased as man with man to dwell, Jesus our Emmanuel!
   Hark! The herald angels sing, "Glory to the newborn King!"

3. Hail, the heav'n born Prince of Peace! Hail, the Son of Righteousness!
   Light and life to all He brings, ris'n with healing in His wings.
   Mild He lays His glory by. Born that man no more may die.
   Born to raise the sons of earth, born to give them second birth.
   Hark! The herald angels sing, "Glory to the newborn King!"

I Saw Three Ships

Traditional English Carol

Verse
Moderately fast

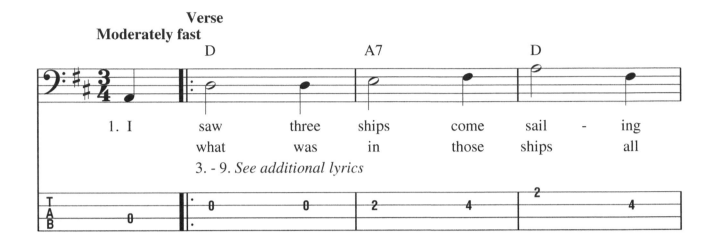

1. I saw three ships come sail - ing
   what was in come those ships all

3. - 9. *See additional lyrics*

in on Christ - mas day, on Christ - mas
three, on Christ - mas day, on Christ - mas

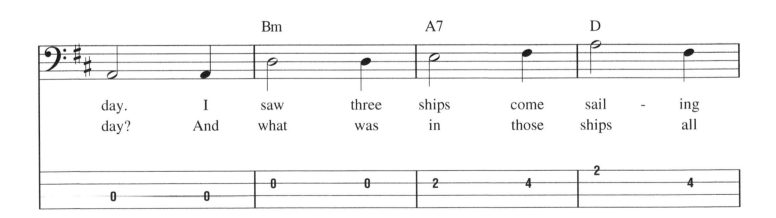

day. I saw three ships come sail - ing
day? And what was in those ships all

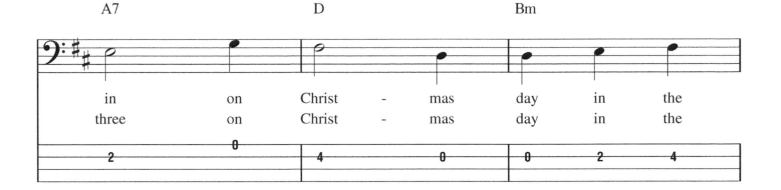

A7		D		Bm		
in	on	Christ	- mas	day	in	the
three	on	Christ	- mas	day	in	the

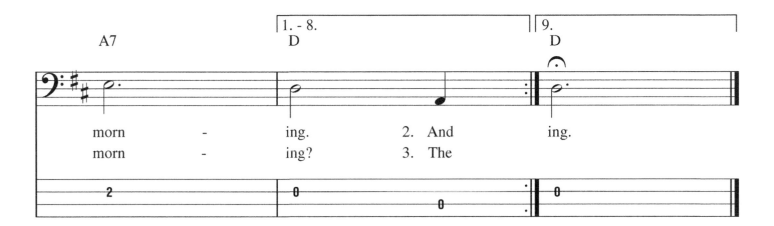

A7   1. - 8. D   9. D

morn	-	ing.	2. And	ing.
morn	-	ing?	3. The	

Additional Lyrics

3. The Virgin Mary and Christ were there on Christmas day, on Christmas day.
   The Virgin Mary and Christ were there on Christmas day in the morning.

4. Pray, whither sailed those ships all three on Christmas day, on Christmas day?
   Pray, whither sailed those ships all three on Christmas day in the morning?

5. Oh, they sailed into Bethlehem on Christmas day, on Christmas day.
   Oh, they sailed into Bethlehem on Christmas day in the morning.

6. And all the bells on earth shall ring on Christmas day, on Christmas day.
   And all the bells on earth shall ring on Christmas day in the morning.

7. And all the angels in heaven shall sing on Christmas day, on Christmas day.
   And all the angels in heaven shall sing on Christmas day in the morning.

8. And all the souls on earth shall sing on Christmas day, on Christmas day.
   And all the souls on earth shall sing on Christmas day in the morning.

9. Then let us all rejoice again on Christmas day, on Christmas day.
   Then let us all rejoice again on Christmas day in the morning.

It Came Upon the Midnight Clear

Words by Edmund H. Sears
Traditional English Melody
Adapted by Arthur Sullivan

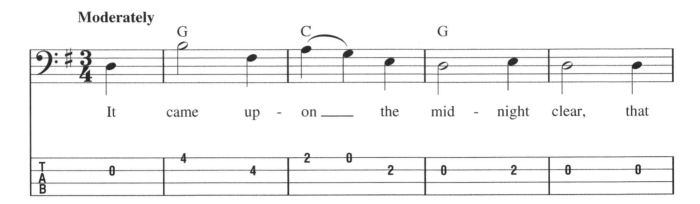

It came up - on ___ the mid - night clear, that

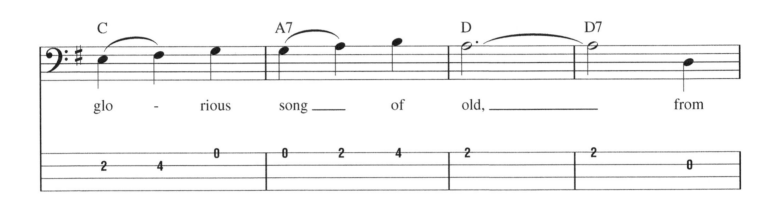

glo - rious song ___ of old, _____ from

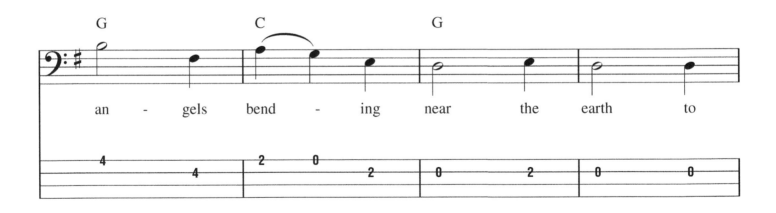

an - gels bend - ing near the earth to

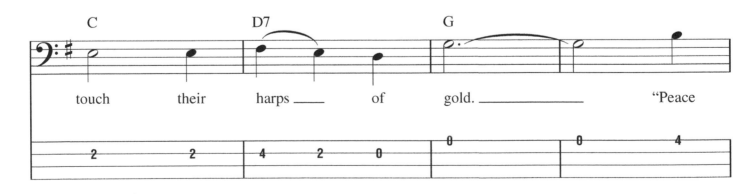

touch their harps ___ of gold. _____ "Peace

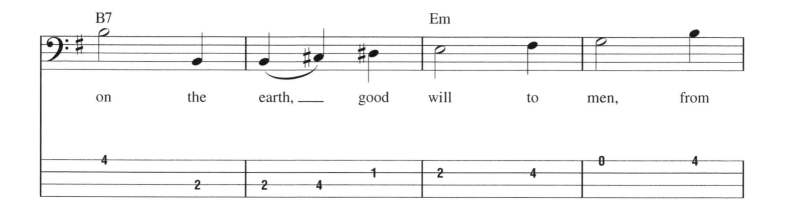

on the earth, ___ good will to men, from

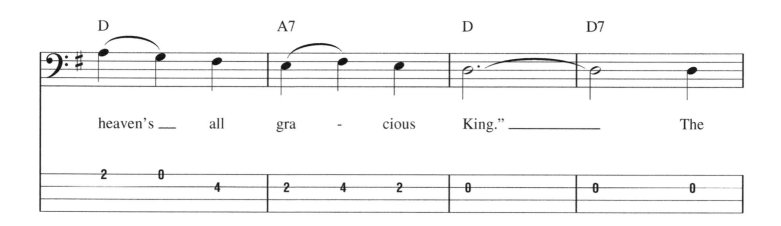

heaven's ___ all gra - cious King." _____ The

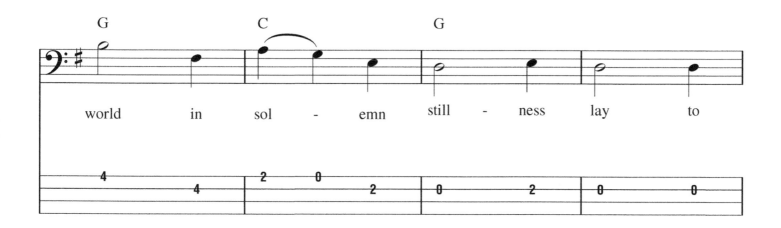

world in sol - emn still - ness lay to

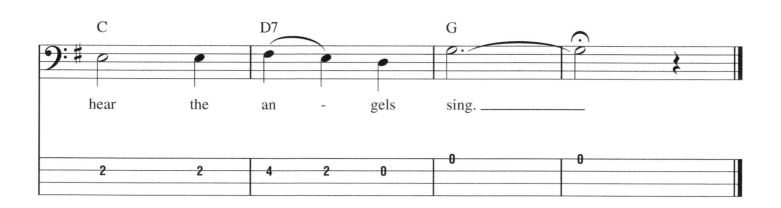

hear the an - gels sing. _____

Jingle Bells

Words and Music by J. Pierpont

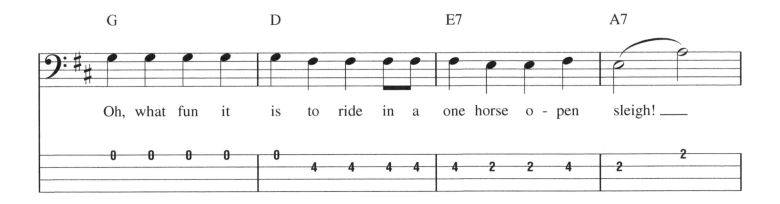

Oh, what fun it is to ride in a one horse o - pen sleigh! ___

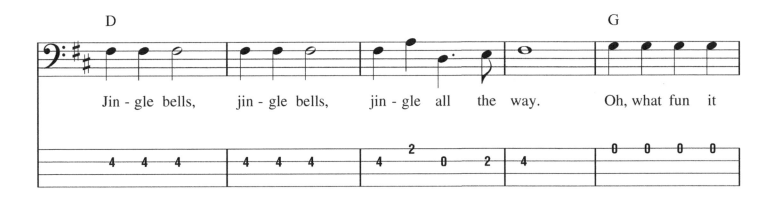

Jin - gle bells, jin - gle bells, jin - gle all the way. Oh, what fun it

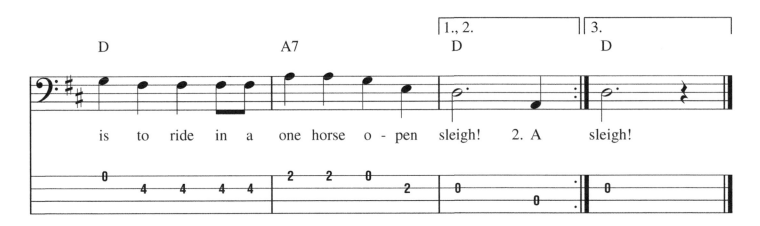

is to ride in a one horse o - pen sleigh! 2. A sleigh!

Additional Lyrics

2. A day or two ago, I thought I'd take a ride,
   And soon Miss Fannie Bright was sitting by my side.
   The horse was lean and lank,
   Misfortune seemed his lot.
   He got into a drifted bank and we, we got upshot! Oh!

3. Now the ground is white, go it while you're young.
   Take the girls tonight and sing this sleighing song.
   Just get a bobtail bay,
   Two-forty for his speed.
   Then hitch him to an open sleigh and crack, you'll take the lead! Oh!

Joy to the World

Words by Isaac Watts
Music by George Frideric Handel
Adapted by Lowell Mason

Verse
Moderately fast

1. Joy to the world! The Lord is come. Let
2. Joy to the world! The Savior reigns. Let
3., 4. *See additional lyrics*

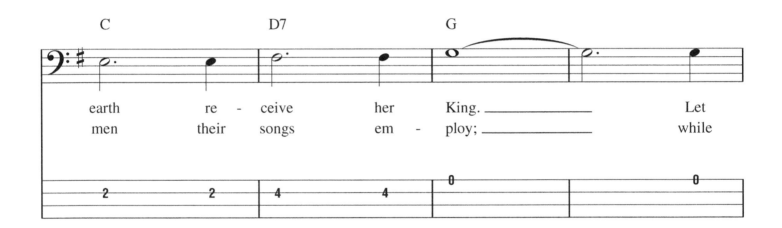

earth re - ceive her King. _____ Let
men their songs em - ploy; _____ while

ev - 'ry ___ heart ____ pre - pare ___ Him ___ room, ____ and
fields ___ and ___ floods, ____ rocks, hills, ___ and ___ plains ____ re -

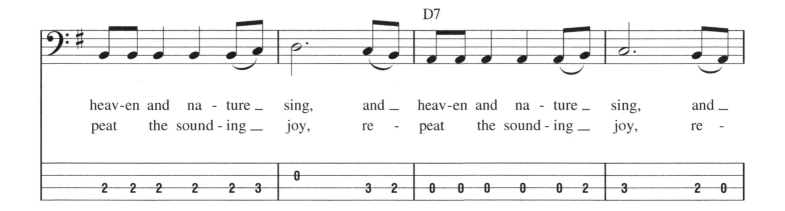

heav-en and na - ture _ sing,   and _ heav-en and na - ture _ sing,   and _
peat   the sound - ing _ joy,   re - peat   the sound - ing _ joy,   re -

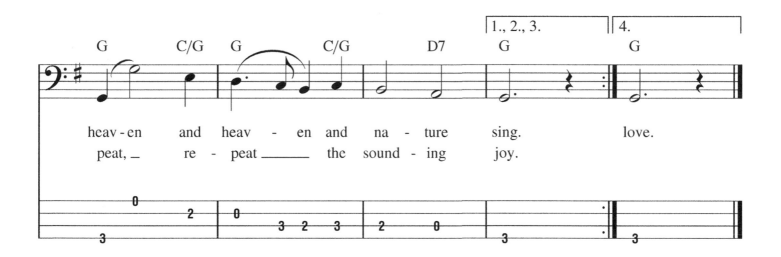

heav - en   and   heav - en and na - ture sing.   love.
peat, _   re - peat   the   sound - ing   joy.

Additional Lyrics

3. No more let sin and sorrow grow,
   Nor thorns infest the ground.
   He comes to make His blessings flow
   Far as the curse is found,
   Far as the curse is found,
   Far as, far as the curse is found.

4. He rules the world with truth and grace,
   And makes the nations prove
   The glories of His righteousness,
   And wonders of His love,
   And wonders of His love,
   And wonders, wonders of His love.

O Christmas Tree

Traditional German Carol

Additional Lyrics

2. O Christmas tree! O Christmas tree,
Much pleasure doth thou bring me!
O Christmas tree! O Christmas tree,
Much pleasure does thou bring me!
For every year the Christmas tree
Brings to us all both joy and glee.
O Christmas tree! O Christmas tree,
Much pleasure doth thou bring me!

3. O Christmas tree! O Christmas tree,
Thy candles shine out brightly!
O Christmas tree, O Christmas tree,
Thy candles shine out brightly!
Each bough doth hold its tiny light
That makes each toy to sparkle bright.
O Christmas tree, O Christmas tree,
Thy candles shine out brightly.

O Holy Night

French Words by Placide Cappeau
English Words by John S. Dwight
Music by Adolphe Adam

Verse

Moderately

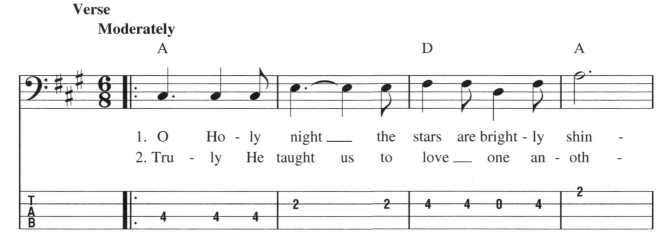

1. O Ho - ly night ___ the stars are bright - ly shin -
2. Tru - ly He taught us to love ___ one an - oth -

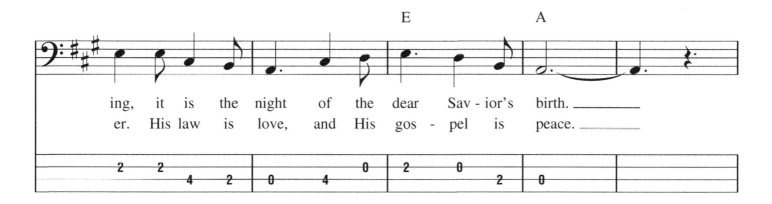

ing, it is the night of the dear Sav - ior's birth. ___
er. His law is love, and His gos - pel is peace. ___

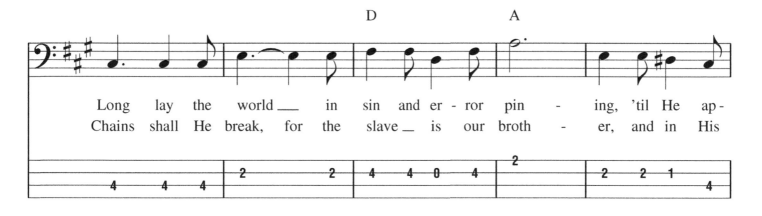

Long lay the world ___ in sin and er - ror pin - ing, 'til He ap -
Chains shall He break, for the slave ___ is our broth - er, and in His

peared and the soul felt its worth. ___ A thrill of hope the
name all op - pres - sion shall cease. ___ Sweet hymns of joy in

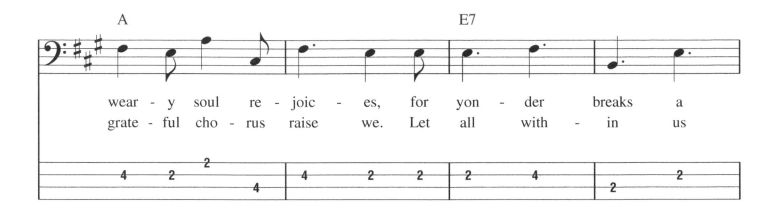

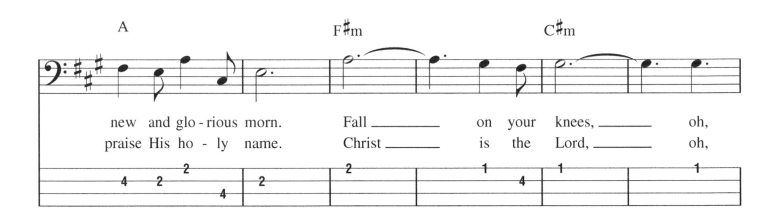

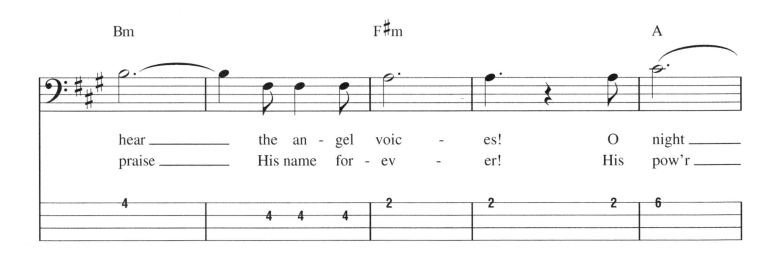

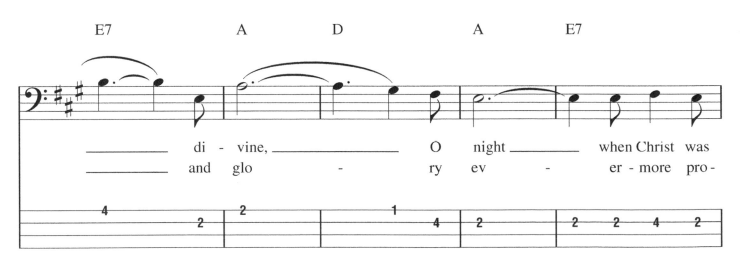

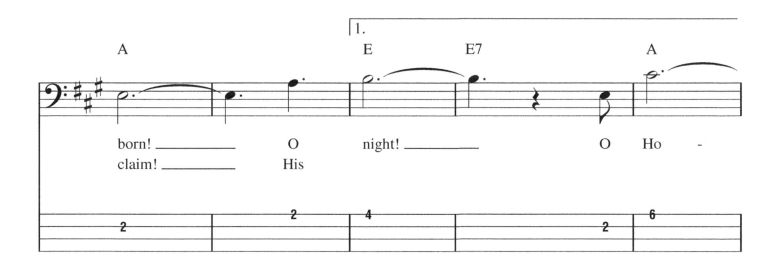

born! _____ O night! _____ O Ho -
claim! _____ His

- ly night! O night di - vine! _____

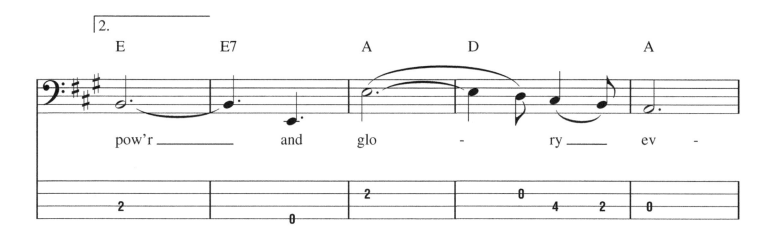

pow'r _____ and glo - ry _____ ev -

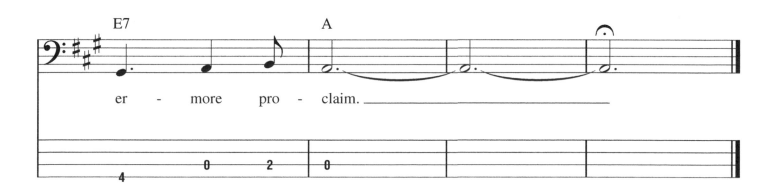

er - more pro - claim. _____

O Come, All Ye Faithful

(Adeste Fideles)

Music by John Francis Wade
Latin Words translated by Frederick Oakeley

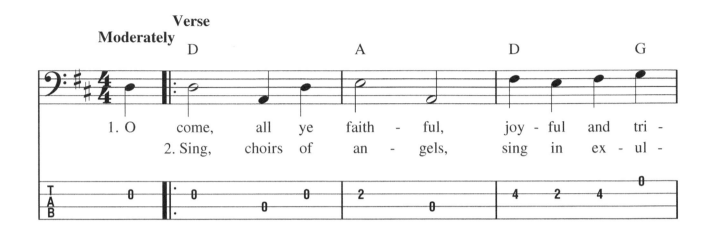

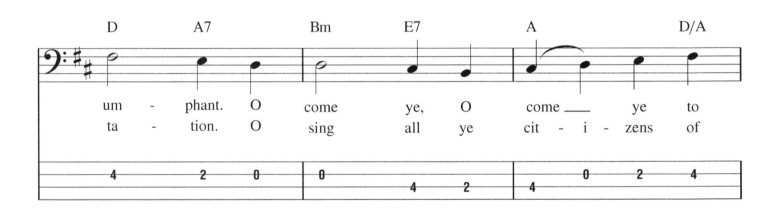

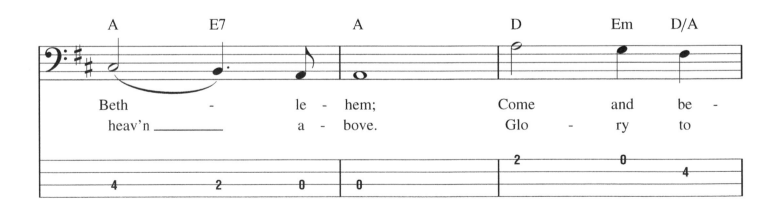

O Come, O Come Immanuel

Plainsong, 13th Century
Words translated by John M. Neale and Henry S. Coffin

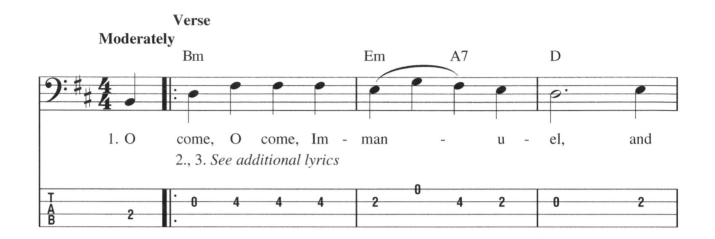

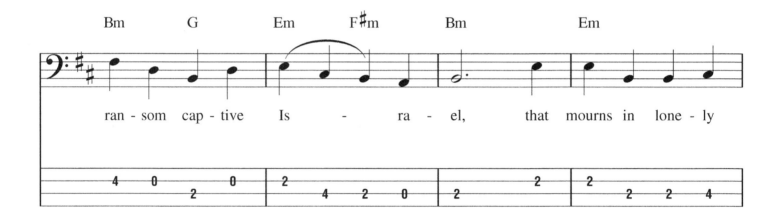

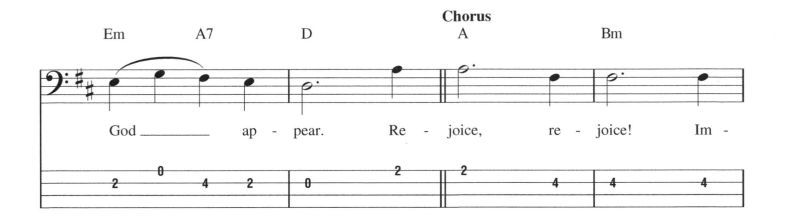

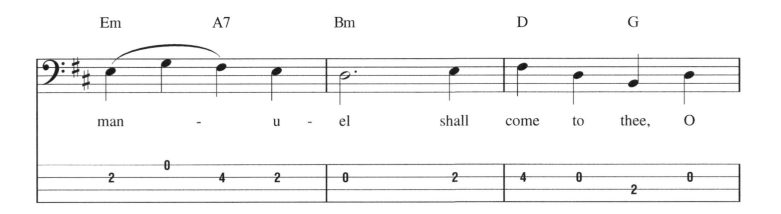

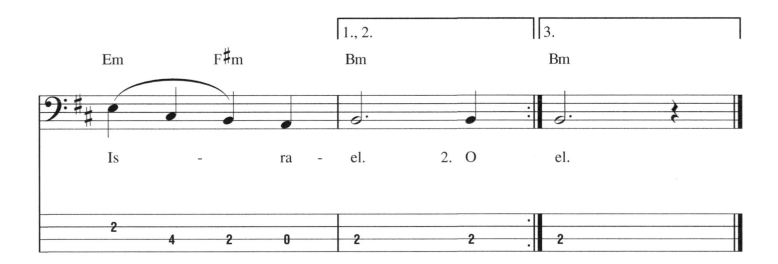

Additional Lyrics

2. O come, Thou Wisdom from on high,
   And order all things far and nigh;
   To us, the path of knowledge show
   And cause us in her ways to go.

3. O come, Desire of nations, bind
   All people in one heart and mind;
   Bid envy, strife, and quarrel's cease;
   Fill the whole world with heaven's peace.

O Little Town of Bethlehem

Words by Phillips Brooks
Music by Lewis H. Redner

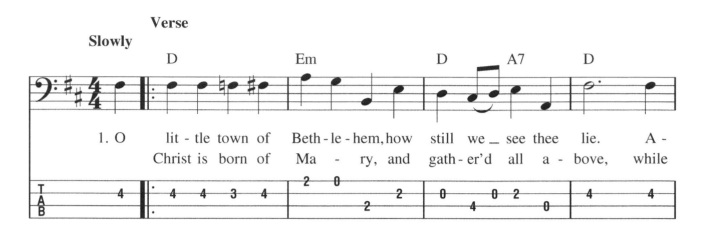

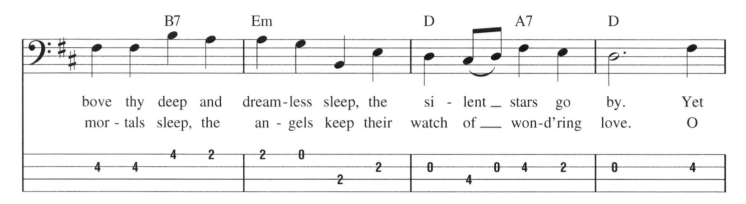

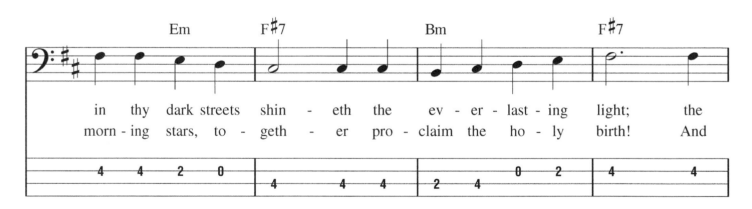

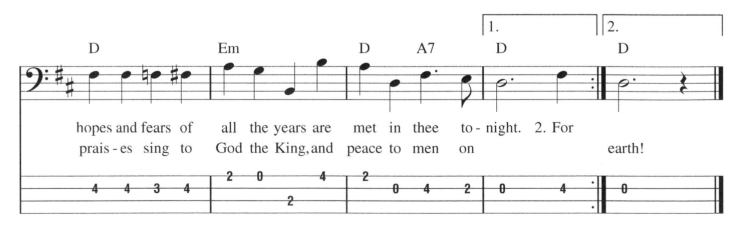

Silent Night

Words by Joseph Mohr
Translated by John F. Young
Music by Franz X. Gruber

Verse
Moderately slow

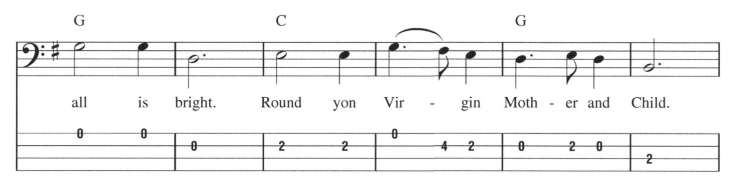

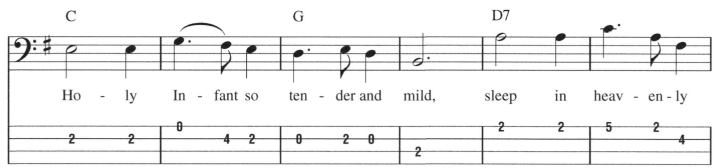

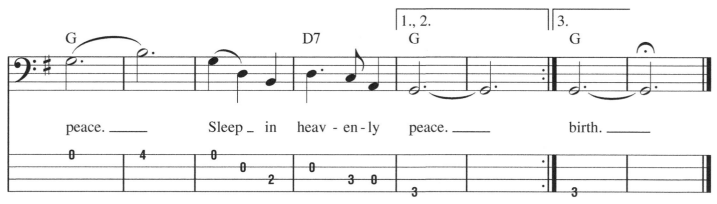

Additional Lyrics

2. Silent night, holy night!
   Shepherds quake at the sight.
   Glories stream from heaven afar.
   Heavenly hosts sing Alleluia.
   Christ the Savior is born!
   Christ the Savior is born!

3. Silent night, holy night!
   Son of God, love's pure light.
   Radiant beams from thy holy face
   With the dawn of redeeming grace,
   Jesus Lord at Thy birth.
   Jesus Lord at Thy birth.

Up on the Housetop

Words and Music by B.R. Handy

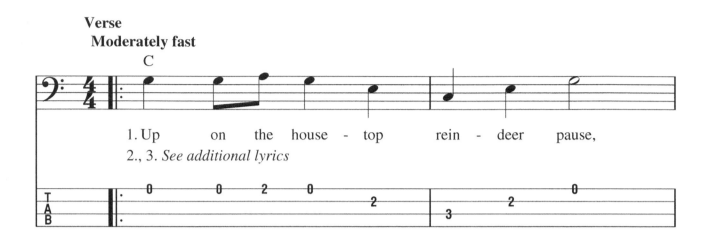

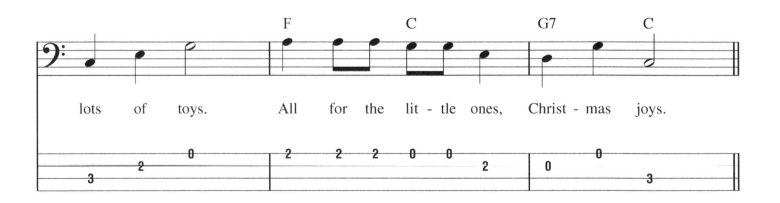

Chorus

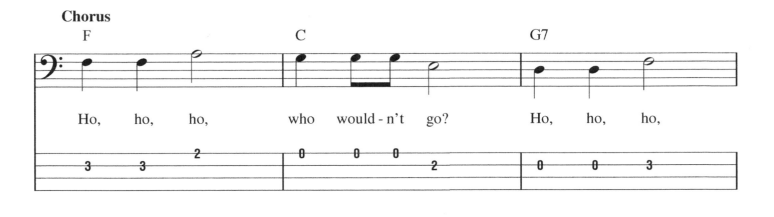

Ho, ho, ho, who would-n't go? Ho, ho, ho,

who would-n't go? _____ Up on the house - top, click, click, click.

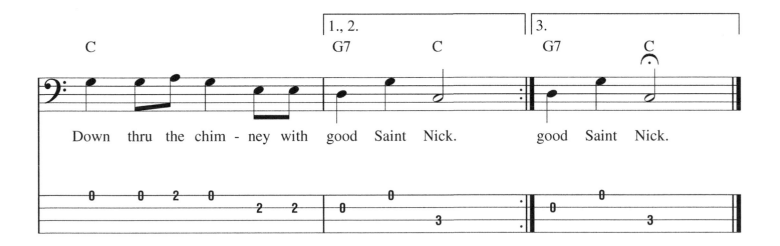

Down thru the chim - ney with good Saint Nick. good Saint Nick.

Additional Lyrics

2. First comes the stocking of little Nell,
   Oh, dear Santa, fill it well.
   Give her a dollie that laughs and cries,
   One that will open and shut her eyes.

3. Next comes the stocking of little Will,
   Oh, just see what a glorious fill!
   Here is a hammer and lots of tacks,
   Also a ball and a whip that cracks.

We Three Kings of Orient Are

Words and Music by John H. Hopkins, Jr.

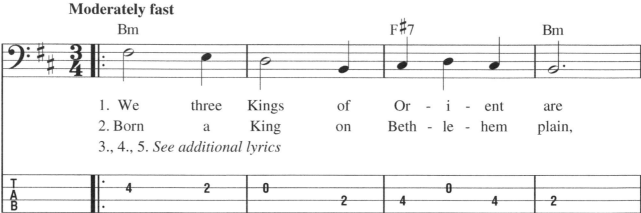

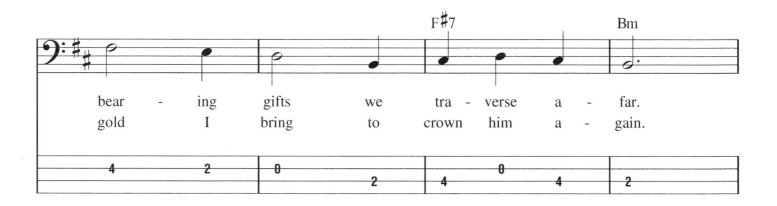

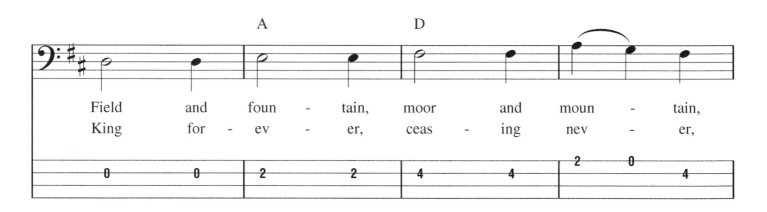

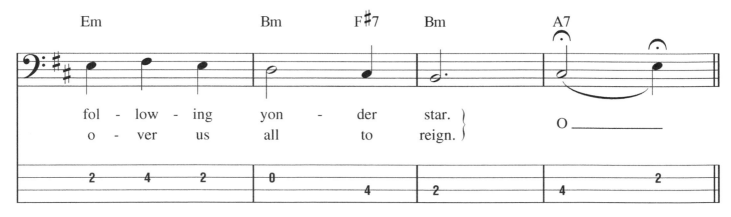

Additional Lyrics

3. Frankincense to offer have I;
   Incense owns a Deity nigh;
   Prayer and praising, all men raising,
   Worship Him, God most high.

4. Myrrh is mine: it's bitter perfume
   Breathes a life of gathering gloom:
   Sorrowing, sighing, bleeding, dying;
   Sealed in the stone-cold tomb.

5. Glorious now, behold Him arise,
   King and God, and Sacrifice!
   Heav'n sings alleluia,
   Alleluia the earth replies:

What Child Is This?

Words by William C. Dix
16th Century English Melody

Verse
Moderately slow

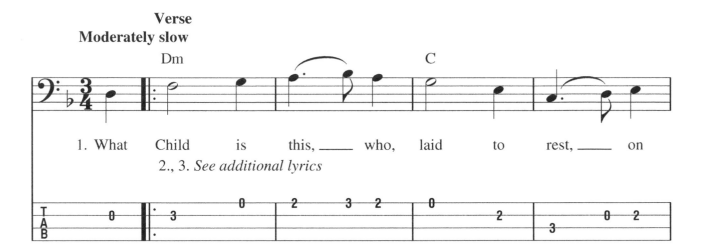

1. What Child is this, ____ who, laid to rest, ____ on
2., 3. *See additional lyrics*

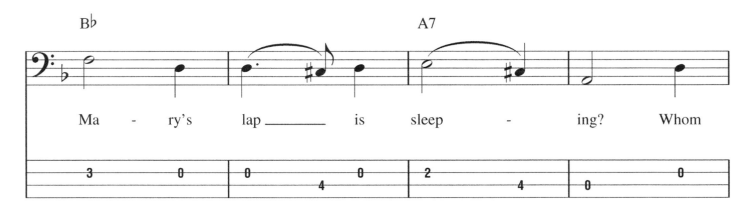

Ma - ry's lap _____ is sleep - ing? Whom

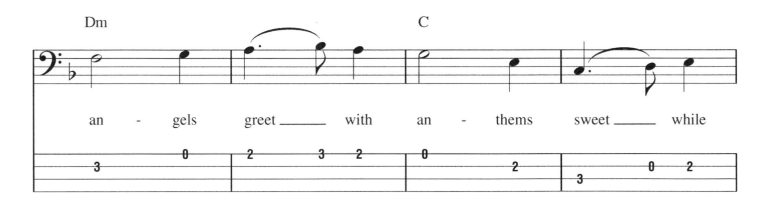

an - gels greet _____ with an - thems sweet _____ while

shep - herds watch _____ are keep - ing?

Chorus

This, this _____ is Christ the King, _____ whom

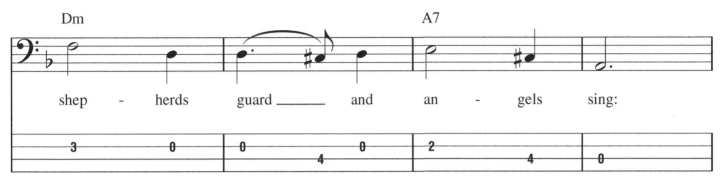

shep - herds guard _____ and an - gels sing:

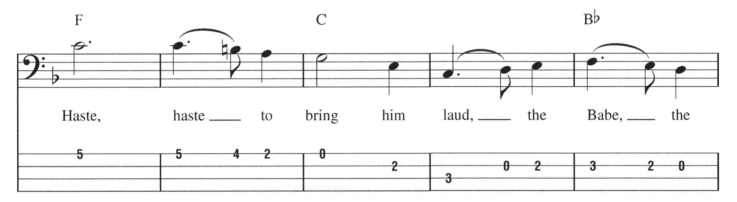

Haste, haste _____ to bring him laud, _____ the Babe, _____ the

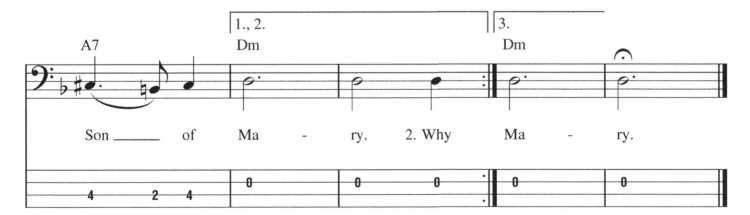

Son _____ of Ma - ry. 2. Why Ma - ry.

Additional Lyrics

2. Why lies He in such mean estate
   Where ox and ass are feeding?
   Good Christian, fear, for sinners here
   The silent word is pleading.

3. So bring Him incense, gold and myrrh.
   Come, peasant King, to own Him.
   The King of Kings salvation brings,
   Let loving hearts enthrone Him.

43

We Wish You a Merry Christmas

Traditional English Folksong

BASS BUILDERS

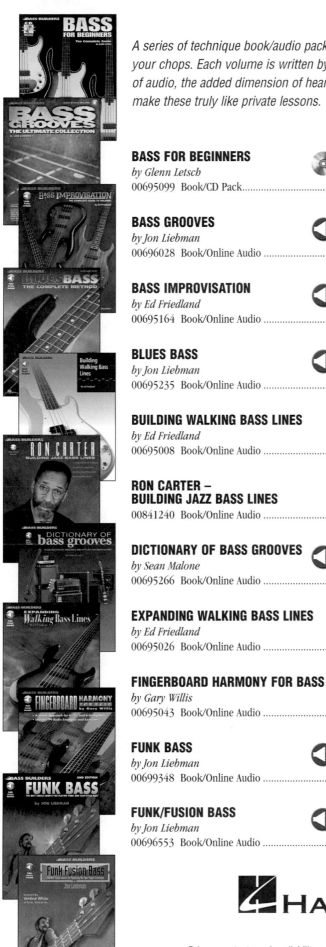

A series of technique book/audio packages created for the purposeful building and development of your chops. Each volume is written by an expert in that particular technique. And with the inclusion of audio, the added dimension of hearing exactly how to play particular grooves and techniques make these truly like private lessons.

BASS FOR BEGINNERS
by Glenn Letsch
00695099 Book/CD Pack.............................$19.95

BASS GROOVES
by Jon Liebman
00696028 Book/Online Audio $19.99

BASS IMPROVISATION
by Ed Friedland
00695164 Book/Online Audio $19.99

BLUES BASS
by Jon Liebman
00695235 Book/Online Audio $19.99

BUILDING WALKING BASS LINES
by Ed Friedland
00695008 Book/Online Audio $19.99

RON CARTER –
BUILDING JAZZ BASS LINES
00841240 Book/Online Audio $19.99

DICTIONARY OF BASS GROOVES
by Sean Malone
00695266 Book/Online Audio $14.95

EXPANDING WALKING BASS LINES
by Ed Friedland
00695026 Book/Online Audio $19.99

FINGERBOARD HARMONY FOR BASS
by Gary Willis
00695043 Book/Online Audio $17.99

FUNK BASS
by Jon Liebman
00699348 Book/Online Audio $19.99

FUNK/FUSION BASS
by Jon Liebman
00696553 Book/Online Audio $24.99

HIP-HOP BASS
by Josquin des Prés
00695589 Book/Online Audio $15.99

JAZZ BASS
by Ed Friedland
00695084 Book/Online Audio $17.99

JERRY JEMMOTT –
BLUES AND RHYTHM &
BLUES BASS TECHNIQUE
00695176 Book/CD Pack.............................$24.99

JUMP 'N' BLUES BASS
by Keith Rosier
00695292 Book/Online Audio $17.99

THE LOST ART OF COUNTRY BASS
by Keith Rosier
00695107 Book/Online Audio $19.99

PENTATONIC SCALES FOR BASS
by Ed Friedland
00696224 Book/Online Audio $19.99

REGGAE BASS
by Ed Friedland
00695163 Book/Online Audio $16.99

'70S FUNK & DISCO BASS
by Josquin des Prés
00695614 Book/Online Audio $16.99

SIMPLIFIED SIGHT-READING FOR BASS
by Josquin des Prés
00695085 Book/Online Audio $17.99

6-STRING BASSICS
by David Gross
00695221 Book/Online Audio $14.99

HAL•LEONARD®
halleonard.com
Prices, contents and availability subject to change without notice; All prices are listed in U.S. funds

BASS RECORDED VERSIONS

Bass Recorded Versions feature authentic transcriptions written in standard notation and tablature for bass guitar. This series features complete bass lines from the classics to contemporary superstars.

25 Essential Rock Bass Classics
00690210 / $19.99

Avenged Sevenfold – Nightmare
00691054 / $19.99

The Beatles – Abbey Road
00128336 / $24.99

The Beatles – 1962-1966
00690556 / $19.99

The Beatles – 1967-1970
00690557 / $24.99

Best of Bass Tab
00141806 / $17.99

The Best of Blink 182
00690549 / $18.99

Blues Bass Classics
00690291 / $22.99

Boston – Bass Collection
00690935 / $19.95

Stanley Clarke – Collection
00672307 / $22.99

Dream Theater – Bass Anthology
00119345 / $29.99

Funk Bass Bible
00690744 / $27.99

Hard Rock Bass Bible
00690746 / $22.99

Jimi Hendrix – Are You Experienced?
00690371 / $17.95

Jimi Hendrix – Bass Tab Collection
00160505 / $24.99

Iron Maiden – Bass Anthology
00690867 / $24.99

Jazz Bass Classics
00102070 / $19.99

The Best of Kiss
00690080 / $22.99

Lynyrd Skynyrd – All-Time Greatest Hits
00690956 / $24.99

Bob Marley – Bass Collection
00690568 / $24.99

Mastodon – Crack the Skye
00691007 / $19.99

Megadeth – Bass Anthology
00691191 / $22.99

Metal Bass Tabs
00103358 / $22.99

Best of Marcus Miller
00690811 / $29.99

Motown Bass Classics
00690253 / $19.99

Muse – Bass Tab Collection
00123275 / $22.99

Nirvana – Bass Collection
00690066 / $19.99

Nothing More – Guitar & Bass Collection
00265439 / $24.99

The Offspring – Greatest Hits
00690809 / $17.95

The Essential Jaco Pastorius
00690420 / $22.99

Jaco Pastorius – Greatest Jazz Fusion Bass Player
00690421 / $24.99

Pearl Jam – Ten
00694882 / $22.99

Pink Floyd – Dark Side of the Moon
00660172 / $19.99

The Best of Police
00660207 / $24.99

Pop/Rock Bass Bible
00690747 / $24.99

Queen – The Bass Collection
00690065 / $22.99

R&B Bass Bible
00690745 / $24.99

Rage Against the Machine
00690248 / $22.99

Red Hot Chili Peppers – BloodSugarSexMagik
00690064 / $22.99

Red Hot Chili Peppers – By the Way
00690585 / $24.99

Red Hot Chili Peppers – Californication
00690390 / $22.99

Red Hot Chili Peppers – Greatest Hits
00690675 / $22.99

Red Hot Chili Peppers – I'm with You
00691167 / $22.99

Red Hot Chili Peppers – One Hot Minute
00690091 / $22.99

Red Hot Chili Peppers – Stadium Arcadium
00690853 / Book Only $24.95

Rock Bass Bible
00690446 / $22.99

Rolling Stones – Bass Collection
00690256 / $24.99

Royal Blood
00151826 / $24.99

Rush – The Spirit of Radio: Greatest Hits 1974-1987
00323856 / $24.99

Best of Billy Sheehan
00173972 / $24.99

Slap Bass Bible
00159716 / $29.99

Sly & The Family Stone for Bass
00109733 / $24.99

Best of Yes
00103044 / $24.99

Best of ZZ Top for Bass
00691069 / $24.99

Visit Hal Leonard Online at
www.halleonard.com

Prices, contents & availability subject to change without notice.
Some products may not be available outside the U.S.A.

HAL LEONARD BASS METHOD

METHOD BOOKS

by Ed Friedland

BOOK 1 - 2ND EDITION
Book 1 teaches: tuning; playing position; musical symbols; notes within the first five frets; common bass lines, patterns and rhythms; rhythms through eighth notes; playing tips and techniques; more than 100 great songs, riffs and examples; and more! The audio includes 44 full-band tracks for demonstration or play-along.
00695067 Book Only $9.99
00695068 Book/Online Audio................................ $14.99
01100122 Deluxe - Book/Online Audio/Video $19.99

BOOK 2 - 2ND EDITION
Book 2 continues where Book 1 left off and teaches: the box shape; moveable boxes; notes in fifth position; major and minor scales; the classic blues line; the shuffle rhythm; tablature; and more!
00695069 Book Only.. $9.99
00695070 Book/Online Audio................................ $14.99

BOOK 3 - 2ND EDITION
With the third book, progressing students will learn more great songs, riffs and examples; sixteenth notes; playing off chord symbols; slap and pop techniques; hammer-ons and pull-offs; playing different styles and grooves; and more.
00695071 Book Only $9.99
00695072 Book/Online Audio................................ $14.99

COMPOSITE - 2ND EDITION
This money-saving edition contains Books 1, 2 and 3.
00695073 Book Only... $19.99
00695074 Book/Online Audio................................ $27.99

DVD
Play your favorite songs in no time with this DVD! Covers: tuning, notes in first through third position, rhythms through eighth notes, fingerstyle and pick playing, 4/4 and 3/4 time, and more! Includes 6 full songs and on-screen music notation. 68 minutes.
00695849 DVD $19.95

BASS FOR KIDS
by Chad Johnson
Bass for Kids is a fun, easy course that teaches children to play bass guitar faster than ever before. Popular songs such as "Crazy Train," "Every Breath You Take," "A Hard Day's Night" and "Wild Thing" keep kids motivated, and the clean, simple page layouts ensure their attention remains focused on one concept at a time.
00696449 Book/Online Audio $14.99

REFERENCE BOOKS

BASS SCALE FINDER
by Chad Johnson
Learn to use the entire fretboard with the *Bass Scale Finder*. This book contains over 1,300 scale diagrams for the most important 17 scale types.
00695781 6" x 9" Edition.....................................$9.99
00695778 9" x 12" Edition..................................$10.99

BASS ARPEGGIO FINDER
by Chad Johnson
This extensive reference guide lays out over 1,300 arpeggio shapes. 28 different qualities are covered for each key, and each quality is presented in four different shapes.
00695817 6" x 9" Edition.....................................$9.99
00695816 9" x 12" Edition...................................$9.99

MUSIC THEORY FOR BASSISTS
by Sean Malone
Acclaimed bassist and composer Sean Malone will explain the written language of music, using easy-to-understand terms and concepts, diagrams, and much more. The audio provides 96 tracks of examples, demonstrations, and play-alongs.
00695756 Book/Online Audio $19.99

STYLE BOOKS

BASS LICKS
by Ed Friedland
This comprehensive supplement to any bass method will help students learn over 200 great bass licks, lines and grooves in many rhythmic styles. *Bass Licks* illustrates how simple melodic patterns can become the springboard for group improvisation or the foundation of a song.
00696035 Book/Online Audio $15.99

BASS LINES
by Matt Scharfglass
500 expertly written bass lines, riffs and fills in a wide variety of musical genres are included in this comprehensive collection to help players expand their bass vocabulary. The examples cover many tempos, keys and feels, and include easy bass lines for beginners on up to advanced riffs for more experienced bassists.
00148194 Book/Online Audio $22.99

BLUES BASS
by Ed Friedland
Learn to play studying the songs of B.B. King, Stevie Ray Vaughan, Muddy Waters, Albert King, the Allman Brothers, T-Bone Walker, and many more. Learn riffs from blues classics including: Born Under a Bad Sign • Hideaway • Hoochie Coochie Man • Killing Floor • Pride and Joy • Sweet Home Chicago • The Thrill Is Gone • and more.
00695870 Book/Online Audio $17.99

COUNTRY BASS
by Glenn Letsch
21 songs, including: Act Naturally • Boot Scootin' Boogie • Crazy • Honky Tonk Man • Love You Out Loud • Luckenbach, Texas (Back to the Basics of Love) • No One Else on Earth • Ring of Fire • Southern Nights • Streets of Bakersfield • Whose Bed Have Your Boots Been Under? • and more.
00695928 Book/Online Audio $22.99

FRETLESS BASS
by Chris Kringel
18 songs, including: Bad Love • Continuum • Even Flow • Everytime You Go Away • Hocus Pocus • I Could Die for You • Jelly Roll • King of Pain • Kiss of Life • Lady in Red • Tears in Heaven • Very Early • What I Am • White Room • more.
00695850...$22.99

FUNK BASS
by Chris Kringel
This is your complete guide to learning the basics of grooving and soloing funk bass. Songs include: Can't Stop • I'll Take You There • Let's Groove • Stay • What Is Hip • and more.
00695792 Book/Online Audio.............................. $22.99

R&B BASS
by Glenn Letsch
This book/audio pack uses actual classic R&B, Motown, soul and funk songs to teach you how to groove in the style of James Jamerson, Bootsy Collins, Bob Babbitt, and many others. The 19 songs include: For Once in My Life • Knock on Wood • Mustang Sally • Respect • Soul Man • Stand by Me • and more.
00695823 Book/Online Audio $19.99

ROCK BASS
by Sean Malone
This book/audio pack uses songs from a myriad of rock genres to teach the key elements of rock bass. Includes: Another One Bites the Dust • Beast of Burden • Money • Roxanne • Smells like Teen Spirit • and more.
00695801 Book/Online Audio................................ $22.99

SUPPLEMENTARY SONGBOOKS

These great songbooks correlate with Books 1-3 of the *Hal Leonard Bass Method*, giving students great songs to play while they're still learning! The audio tracks include great accompaniment and demo tracks.

EASY POP BASS LINES
20 great songs that students in Book 1 can master. Includes: Come as You Are • Crossfire • Great Balls of Fire • Imagine • Surfin' U.S.A. • Takin' Care of Business • Wild Thing • and more.
00695809 Book/Online Audio.............................. $16.99

MORE EASY POP BASS LINES
20 great songs for Level 2 students. Includes: Bad, Bad Leroy Brown • Crazy Train • I Heard It Through the Grapevine • My Generation • Pride and Joy • Ramblin' Man • Summer of '69 • and more.
00695819 Book Only... $14.99
00695818 Book/Online Audio.............................. $16.99

EVEN MORE EASY POP BASS LINES
20 great songs for Level 3 students, including: ABC • Another One Bites the Dust • Brick House • Come Together • Higher Ground • Iron Man • The Joker • Sweet Emotion • Under Pressure • more.
00695821 Book.. $14.99
00695820 Book/Online Audio.............................. $16.99

Visit Hal Leonard online at
www.halleonard.com